# ABOUT YOGA DIET

# ABOUT YOGA
# DIET

*by*

## HARVEY DAY

THORSONS PUBLISHERS LIMITED

37/38 Margaret Street, London, W.1

First published October 1969

SBN 7225 0150 1

*Made and printed in Great Britain by
Weatherbys Printers, Denington Estate,
Wellingborough*

# CONTENTS

*Yogi* or *Yogin*

One who practises yoga. Feminine: *yogini*

# CHAPTER ONE

# SHOULD A YOGI EAT MEAT?

WHEN, six thousand years ago, yoga was being developed men did not set such store on diet as some do now. The science of dietetics was not thought of. There was no need for it.

India was thickly forested. The soil was fertile. Rivers and streams brought pure water in abundance. Bananas, mangoes, jack-fruit, grapes and an endless variety of indigenous fruits and nuts satisfied the people's needs. There were many kinds of peas, vegetables, herbs and spices; wheat in the north and nort-west; rice and yams in the east and south. Fish abounded in rivers, lakes and in the sea. Milk and milk products were consumed by all; honey was plentiful. For those who ate flesh there was mutton, beef, venison, pork, game and fish.

Ancient India flowed with milk and honey and was not impoverished as many vast tracts are now. Since then large areas of forest have been felled for timber and fuel, denuding the land of protective green cover. Winds have lifted the top soil and carried it away, creating dust bowls and deserts. Many rivers dried up completely or changed their courses, altering the ecology, so that today the land cannot sustain the millions who live there.

## All Foods Were Protective

In those early days every morsel consumed was grown in natural humus, which built up resistance to disease. It did not matter what one ate, food contained essential minerals and vitamins and the natives were healthy and energetic.

*The Hunzas*

All over ancient India people must have lived as the Hunzas did till forty or fifty years ago, when McCarrison* visited them and was astounded by their health, vitality and immunity to disease.

"My own experience," he wrote, "provides an example of a race, unsurpassed in perfection of physique and in freedom from disease in general, whose sole food consists to this day, of grains, vegetables and fruits, with a certain amount of milk and butter, and meat only on feast days. I refer to the people of the State of Hunza, situated in the extreme northernmost part of India. So limited is the land available for cultivation that they can keep little livestock other than goats, which browse on the hills, while the food supply is so restricted that the people, as a rule, do not keep dogs.

"They have, in addition to grains—wheat, barley and maize —an abundant crop of apricots. These they dry in the sun and use very largely in their food. Among these people the span of life is extraordinarily long; and such service as I have been able to render them during some seven years spent in their midst was confined chiefly to the treatment of accidental lesions, the removal of senile cataract, plastic operations for granular eyelids, or the treatment of maladies wholly unconnected with food supply.

"Appendicitis, so common in Europe, was unknown. When the severe nature of the winter in that part of the Himalayas is considered, and the fact that their housing accommodation and conservancy arrangements are of the most primitive, it becomes obvious that the enforced restriction to the unsophisticated foodstuffs of nature is compatible with long life, continued vigour, and perfect physique."

* Major-General Sir Robert McCarrison, C.I.E., M.A., M.D., Ll.D., F.R.C.P.

McCarrison was the first medical man to make a dietary experiment on such a vast scale, using as his laboratory the entire sub-continent of India, and the conclusions he reached are valid to this day.

## The Golden Age

Six thousand years ago the people of India enjoyed a standard of health and vigour that must have been the envy of the ancient world. The population was less than a hundredth of what it is now and there was plenty for all. During the reign of Chandragupta (316-292 B.C.) such a high state of civilization existed that Indians did not need locks on their doors, written contracts were unnecessary, and citizens rarely went to law. Women were chaste (!), men courageous, and both sexes dressed in flowered muslins embroidered with jewels.

## Asoka The Great

His grandson, Asoka, was one of the first kings in history to abjure war altogether and in these two reigns India passed through her Golden Age. Asoka was converted to Buddhism, became a believer in *ahimsa* (non-violence), and as a logical result, a vegetarian. Among the many wise edicts he passed, were:

"Not a single living creature shall be slaughtered and sacrificed.

"Formerly, in the kitchens of his Sacred and Gracious Majesty many hundreds of thousands of living creatures were slaughtered daily for the purpose of making curries. Now, while this religious edict is being inscribed, only three living creatures are slaughtered: two peacocks and a deer; and the deer, not regularly." It was on Asoka's example that most of the people of India renounced the eating of flesh, and to this day yogis and their disciples, together with hundreds of millions of Hindus, are vegetarians. They will not kill in order to live. Many, however, live on milk products, and some will even eat eggs.

## Flesh Is Not Banned

When *chelas* (disciples) are mastering yoga and wander throughout the country in search of experience and humility, they beg for alms, will do any work required of them, and when offered food must accept it, whether vegetable, flesh, fish or fowl, for according to yoga belief all substances come from the same source, to which ultimately they will all return. They take the vow of compassion, however, and refuse to kill or injure, and once they become yogis flesh never enters their lips again. One should not be censorious of meat-eaters; their conscience alone must make them decide whether they will, or will not, eat flesh.

## Vegetarianism

Vegetarianism, from a dietetic point of view, is not part of the yogi's creed because originally there was no need for it, but the true yogi gravitates to vegetarianism because of his compassion for life.

Rama, Krishna, and centuries later Buddha, all ate meat if it was placed before them rather than offend, for offending one's host is a form of injury. The eating of flesh does not make one less spiritual; this lies in the mind. Vegetarians often adopt a "holier-than-thou" attitude which is both priggish and conceited, and many of them are just as cruel, bigoted, violent, filled with hatred, lust, pride, ignorance and prejudice as any carnivorous person. Hitler and Mussolini both professed to be vegetarians!

Nor is there any positive evidence that vegetarians live longer than meat-eaters, though the odds are that they will be freer from disease in middle and old age.

*Why Yoga Is Linked With Vegetarianism*

There are two cogent reasons for the yoga student to become a vegetarian. The first is compassion and a respect for life; the second, that every ingredient for both health and strength comes out of the land and is turned into flesh by an added process, and has to be cooked. Unfired foods are far better for the body, which can be fully developed and brought to a state of perfection by *asanas* (exercises or postures), *pranayama* (special breathing techniques and meditation), and rendered immune to disease. Advanced yogis can eat and drink poisons that would destroy normal people.

Vegetarianism is also healthier than a meat diet. Dr. John Harvey Kellogg, the famous American surgeon, observed that "almost every chronic disease known is directly or indirectly due to the influence of bacterial poisons absorbed from the intestine;"* and Dr. Ch. Bouchard stated in *Auto-Intoxication In Disease*; "If, as demonstrated, the gastro-intestinal tract is the source of the largest number of poisons that cause auto-intoxication, then clearly it is this part of the body that calls for special attention and treatment;" and it is a meat-diet rather than a diet of fruit and vegetables that is liable to cause auto-intoxication.

*Colon Irrigation*

In advanced stages of the disease many methods of colon irrigation are used: the enema or advanced forms of mechanical irrigation are used by physicians and in Nature Cure homes. Naturopaths recommend agar-agar, all-bran, the invariable use of wholemeal bread and flour, bulky and leafy vegetables, B-complex vitamins, and special exercises for strengthening slack stomach muscles.

* *Colon Hygiene*

## The Yoga Method

One need never suffer from auto-intoxication if yoga is embraced. Some five thousand years ago yogis advocated breathing exercises, internal kneading and massage through *uddiya bandha* and *nauli*, exercises for the waist and abdomen, air irrigation (*sthula*, *suska* or *basti*), and water irrigation of the colon (*jalabasti*), which is the natural way of administering an enema. Air is driven out of the lungs by exhaling and powerful muscular action, creating a vacuum, and allowing water to be drawn into the intestines through the anus. This they developed by watching birds and animals closely. *The Lancet* (1883-1884, vol. II, page 960) describes such practices in the animal kingdom. The *asanas* also encourage regular bowel evacuation and so ensure that a healthy colon will always exist.

## Man Is A Herbo-Frugivorous Animal

They also realized through observation and by trial and error, that a meat diet is largely unsuitable because it tends to cause disease after forty; more so than a mixed diet, though a purely fruit, nut, and vegetable diet is best. This has been established by modern medical authorities, but because of modern habits, environment and convenience, a lacto-vegetarian diet is easier to adhere to and very satisfactory because it does not involve the taking of life or cruelty to animals.

## Ancient Hints On Food

Ancient yoga works, such as *Hatha-Yoga Pradipka*, *Gheranda Samhita* and *Siva Samhita* do not agree on all points, but fundamentally there is agreement. Salt is one of the foods discouraged by the yogis. They also set their faces against sharp, sour, very pungent and bitter foods, some of which stimulate unnecessarily, or act as aphrodisiacs. And, they were unanimous in condemning drugs as aids to furthering psychic experience. They were a trifle vague about intoxicating liquors for the making of wines and spirits and the brewing of beer was never brought to an art in India. Fermenting brews were classed as intoxicants, and taboo; they can, of course, be deadly, for only after fermentation has ceased, and the liquid has settled and matured, is it fit for human consumption.

### Dr. C. N. Paul

In *A Treatise On The Yoga Philosophy*, Dr. C. N. Paul says that in terms of measurement, if the quantity of waste over a given period in a vegetarian is 1,000, it will be 1,445 in the case of a person living on a mixed diet, and 2,367 for one on a full-flesh diet. On the subject of quantities, *Markandeyapurana* states that one should finish eating when half the stomach has been filled with food, leaving a quarter for water and the remainder for air, and no more than three meals a day should be eaten: a light meal to break one's fast; a mid-day meal, and a heavier meal in the evening.

### How Much Water Does One Need?

Yoga originated in a tropical country where people drink, of necessity, far more than in Britain, but roughly six pints is sufficient, and for most people this will be made up of the tea, coffee, beer, wines and spirits they drink, the water in fruit, vegetables and soups. The yoga injunction, to drink from a clean spring or river, or sink a well for pure water, obviously cannot apply to modern conditions, where all drinking water is chlorinated and in some places is also fluoridized. The yogis says that a pint of water should be taken at 4 a.m. (before starting daily duties!) as an aid to bowel action and altogether about six pints of water should be drunk. Easy enough when liquid oozes out of the pores in the form of sweat, but not in a chilly clime.

It is possible to get all the water the body needs without drinking a glass of plain water. Few people realize that most fresh fruit contain between 78-85 per cent of water in its purest form, and even dried apples, apricots, peaches, prunes and raisins contain more than 20 per cent, and most vegetables from 80-95 per cent. So if you eat plenty of fresh fruit and salads and drink the normal amount of tea, coffee and other beverages you should get all the water you need. What is more, the water in fruit and vegetables contains the minerals and vitamins to keep you healthy.

Yogis believe in eating and drinking separately and this, curiously enough, is scientifically the right thing to do, because when you chew, an enzyme or ferment called ptyalin is secreted in your saliva, which helps to break down carbohydrates (bread, pastry, biscuits, sugar) and prepares them for digestion. If you eat and sip at the same time the ptyalin doesn't get a chance to do its work and the process of digestion is hampered, and incomplete. This, in middle age and after leads to digestive troubles.

Also, if you eat and drink simultaneously you can eat far more than you can if you eat without drinking; and excess food tends to fatten. That is why dinners and luncheons with wines for separate courses don't make for sound die-tetics. You will relish your food more if you drink either before or after.

# CHAPTER TWO

# FOOD FOR HEALTH

THE idea is prevalent that rich food is good food. Open any coffee-table recipe book costing from four to six guineas and the odds are that most of the recipes urge one to use "a gill of cream" or more, and add sherry or other wines to them. The same with sweets. The recipes are so complicated and take so long to prepare that the basic flavours one should enjoy are often lost.

## Plain Cooking Is Best

Plain cooking is almost invariably the tastiest (not costliest), and the best ingredients the cheapest because every scrap can be eaten. Sir William Temple once said: "The only way for a rich man to be healthy is, by exercise and abstinence, to live as if he were poor."

This does not mean that he must do without the good things in life. They are usually simple and cheap.

There is no better cooking than plain English, or for that matter, Indian, cooking. The idea that Indian curries are complicated and pungent enough to blow off the top of your head, is nonsense. The tastiest curries are not hot; spices are used as preservatives, for their health-giving properties, and for their flavour and piquancy. English people are given fiery curries because Indian *restaurateurs* imagine that is what they want!

So, the first essential is to take the best and finest produce and eat it either raw or conservatively cooked. Health is the result of observation and experience and it was only after centuries that men learnt how to eat in order to keep fit.

*Nature and Health*

Lord Horder, one of our great modern physicians, wrote: "Let me remind you that health does not necessarily depend upon science at all. There were millions of healthy persons living before science, as we understand it today, existed. Though a large number of our forebears died prematurely from diseases that we have learnt to prevent or control, by science, many of them who escaped fatal disease, enjoyed even without the help of science as perfect health as we can ever hope to have. We mustn't mistake the explanation which science gives us as to why these folk were healthy for any supposed scientific methods that kept them healthy. Our ancestors didn't follow any scientific methods. To tell the truth, nature taught men how to be healthy long before science discovered the laws of health."

Which is precisely what the yogis told the world centuries ago, and what naturopaths have repeated for nearly a hundred years.

It is interesting to read what those in the past had to say about food and health. "To keep a good diet", laid down the *Regimen Sanitatis of Salerno* (circa 1100 A.D.), "you should never eat until your stomach (is) clean and void of former meat:" that is, let a fair amount of time elapse between one meal and another.

*Wisdom About Bread*

Thomas Cogan, physician and herbalist, who flourished in the sixteenth century, told those who asked his advice: "Brown bread made of the coarsest of wheat flour, having in it much bran, and that bread which Galen called Autopyros, that is, when meal wholly unsifted, bran and all is made into bread, filleth the belly with the excrements, and shortly descended from the stomach. And beside that it is good for labourers. I have known this experience of it, that such as have been used to fine bread, when they have been costive, by eating brown bread and butter have been made soluble."

Most of us, including doctors, haven't digested that lesson delivered nearly four hundred years ago.

## Moderation The Key

I have always believed in moderation as the key to health and in this am backed by Sir Robert Hutchinson, a former President of the Royal College of Physicians, who while dilating on diet, said: "One swears by wholemeal bread, one by sour milk; vegetarianism is the only road to salvation of some; others insist not only on vegetables alone, but insist on eating them raw. At one time the only thing that matters is calories; at another time they are crazy about vitamins or about roughage.

"The scientific truth may be put quite briefly; eat moderately, have an ordinary mixed diet, and don't worry. I believe in the bodily as well as in the spiritual sphere, that he who would save his life shall lose it."

## Balanced Diet

Finally, Lord Horder again. "Science," he wrote, "is slowly discovering why it is that a mixed diet, containing food that has not been too much *tampered with* in its preparation, makes for health, and why a diet that is not sufficiently mixed, or does not contain *enough fresh food*, makes for ill health. It is because foods that are body builders, body protectors and body workers and warmers are all represented in the mixed diet, and some of them are absent, or only present in too small a degree, in the deficiency diets. In other words, those of our ancestors who were healthy ate what is now called a *balanced diet* without knowing it."

That is precisely what the yogis did centuries ago, perhaps without realizing it. They lived on a balanced diet.

Don't be finicky and faddy. Eat food that you like; that smells good, looks good, and as the TV advertisements say,

"By golly, tastes good!" Enjoy your food and provided the ingredients are grown in compost and aren't tampered with, it will do you far more good than if you ponder over calories and vitamins at every mouthful. Man's taste buds were provided by nature as a guide to health.

# CHAPTER THREE

# VEGETARIANS NEED PROTEIN

ONE of the faults found with vegetarian diets by those who don't know enough about food is that they lack protein. This isn't true. The protein content of average meat is 20 per cent, beef 18 per cent, pork 20 per cent, chicken 21 per cent, sea fish 18 per cent, pike 17 per cent, salmon 20 per cent. Compare this with beans 24 per cent, kidney beans 23.12 per cent, lentils 25.7 per cent., dried Lima beans 18 per cent, dried peas 22.8 per cent, oatmeal 16.05 per cent, rolled oats 16.7 per cent, whole rye 11.5 per cent, whole wheat 13.6 per cent, wheat germ 35.7 per cent, cottage cheese 20.9 per cent, Cheddar type cheese 23.75 per cent, eggs 12.55 per cent, soya beans 34.00 per cent.

Nuts vary tremendously in their protein content: peanuts 29.8 per cent, almonds 21.4 per cent, beechnuts 21.7 per cent, Brazils 17.4 per cent, and walnuts 27.6 per cent.

Dietitians are apt to write off vegetable proteins as "second class", because they don't contain all the amino acids needed for health. Children need ten: arginine, leucine, isoleucine, histidine, lysine, phenylalanine, valine, tryptophane, threonine, and menthionine. Adults can get along with only eight. These conclusions were reached after tests on mice, guinea pigs and other creatures with a short life span and it is probable that we manufacture those lacking from some of the others, as animals do, in our own bodies. Otherwise why would the Hunzas, Sikhs and other north-Indian peoples be among the huskiest in the world? Or the Chinese, who live mainly on the soya bean, be among the toughest and hardiest of nations, noted for their stamina?

## *Vegetarianism*

Some vegetarians, known as Vegans, don't even eat cheese or other milk products because they come from animal sources. They maintain that taking the milk from the cow is an act of cruelty which deprives the calf of its natural sustenance, though after a few months even the calf turns from milk to pasture. Vegans maintain also, that milk is an unnatural food and only humans take it after they have passed the weaning stage. This is not accurate, for cats will lap milk and cream, and even birds and reptiles will do so. Milk products—except for the few who are allergic to them—have been proved to be body-building foods.

## *Mahatma Gandhi—Food Reformer*

Mohandas Karamchand Gandhi, known in the West as Mahatma (Great Soul) Gandhi, the Father of Modern India, not only believed in Yoga, but both he and Prime Minister Nehru practised it. Not many people realize that Gandhi was an ardent food reformer.

"Gandhi", urged one of his boyhood friends, "the British eat meat. If they are to be overcome, we must eat meat, too."

The idea was repugnant to Gandhi, who came from a line of staunch Vaishnavas, and Jainism was strong in Gujerat where he was born. No one in India abhors meat-eating as much as the Vaishnavas and Jains. It is against their principles to take life or even cause physical injury.

When I was a boy, my father, a jute merchant, took me to Cotton Street, Calcutta, when he went to see Marwaris (Jains by religion) on business. They were very rich and sat cross-legged on vast silk-covered *gadis* (divans) worked with golden thread.

They were scrupulously clean but neither silk nor thread of gold has ever inhibited an Indian bug from making a bee line to a juicy human morsel. After an hour or so, when courtesies had been exchanged, sherbet sipped, and perhaps a rich sweetmeat eaten, business would be touched on as if it were a secondary consideration. Then suddenly a bug might start to nip and the victim would clap his hands. Servants would come at a trot, the quilt on which the victim sat would be whisked away, taken to the verandah surrounding the courtyard round which such houses are built, and shaken. For it was against their religion to kill bugs or even harm them. One might well be a bug in the next reincarnation.

It is against this background that one must judge Gandhi as a reformer and an iconoclast. His desire to rid India of British rule (not the British) was greater than his repugnance of flesh food, so the two youths bought some baker's bread (as distinct from *chappattis*) and goat's flesh, repaired to a quiet spot by the river and became carnivori.

After a few morsels Gandhi could eat no more and was sick. That night he dreamt he was devouring flesh and a live goat was bleating inside him. Nevertheless, his determination was so great that he and his friend, who had learnt to cook meat, ate their clandestine meals for a year. Then he found he could no longer deceive his parents and reverted to vegetarianism.

His next ordeal came when he was 18 and left Bombay for Britain where he entered the Middle Temple to read law. On the voyage an Englishman who scorned vegetarianism, took him aside. "It's all very well," he told Gandhi, "as long as the weather is warm, but you will revise your opinion in the Bay of Biscay. It is so cold in England that one cannot possibly live without meat." Gandhi decided then that if he found he could not live without meat he would relinquish his studies and return to India.

## Gandhi—Pioneer of Vegetarianism in London

Nearly seventy years ago the lodgings in which students lived were indeed bleak. When he confessed that he was a

vegetarian his unimaginative landlady fed him on oatmeal
porridge for breakfast and boiled spinach and jam and
bread for lunch. After a while he could stand it no longer so
set out to find a vegetarian restaurant, for his landlady
told him she suspected there were such places in the city.

Eventually after trudging miles he lit on one in Far-
ringdon Street. "The sight of it," he wrote, "filled me with
the same joy that a child feels in getting a thing after its
own heart. Before I entered I noticed books for sale on
exhibition under a glass window near the door. I saw
among them Salt's *Pleas For Vegetarianism*. This I pur-
chased for a shilling and went straight to the dining room.
This was my first hearty meal since my arrival in England.
God had come to my aid."

He digested every word of Salt's book and from that
day determined never to go back on vegetarianism.

## Gandhi's Dietetic Education

Salt's book so whetted his appetite for knowledge of
dietetics that he bought everything on vegetarianism he
could find, among them *The Ethics of Diet* by Howard
Williams, *The Perfect Way in Diet* by Anna Kingsford,
and a score of books and tracts by that pioneer, Dr. T. R.
Allinson. The moment he entered that restaurant proved
to be the turning point of his life.

An Indian friend who thought Gandhi was muddling
his head with a lot of nonsense invited him to a meal at the
Holborn Restaurant, but when the waiter handed him the
menu Gandhi asked if there was any vegetable soup and
wanted to know how the other dishes were made. His
embarrassed friend rebuked him. "If you can't behave
yourself you'd better go." This delighted Gandhi and out he
went, to wait round the corner, and when his friend emerged
they enjoyed the remainder of the evening at a theatre.

At that time there existed a vegetarian society in London,

which published a magazine called *The Vegetarian*. He not only subscribed to it but joined the Society and became one of its pillars. He gave up eating sweets and condiments, tea and coffee, and lived for a period on wholemeal bread and fruit. Later he existed for a fortnight on milk, cheese and eggs. He experimented all the time.

## Gandhi's Vegetarian Society

Then Gandhi started a vegetarian society in Bayswater and invited Dr. Josiah Oldfield, Editor of *The Vegetarian*, to become President and Sir Edwin Arnold, whose *Song Celestial* is a poetical translation of *The Bhagavad Gita*, Vice-President. Gandhi was Secretary, and the Society flourished until he left for India.

He made many vegetarian friends in England and before leaving invited them to a dinner at the Holborn Restaurant. After the meal he addressed them and among other things, said: "I discovered that several vegetarians find it impossible to remain vegetarian because they make food a fetish and because they think that by becoming vegetarians they can eat as much lentils, haricot beans and cheese as they like. Of course, such people cannot keep their health. Observing along those lines I say that a man should eat sparingly and now and then fast . . ."

## Gandhi The Experimenter

For the first six months after returning to India he lived on fruit and nuts only, although his doctors advised him to add milk to his diet. Then he included small quantities of vegetables, such as cucumber, marrow and pumpkin. "The digestions of most people are very often so impaired through a surfeit of cooked fare," he noted, "that one should not be surprised if at first they fail to do justice to raw greens, though I can say from personal experience that no harmful effect need follow if a *tola* (about 180 grains Troy) or two of raw greens are taken with each meal *provided one masticates them thoroughly.*"

## Raw Food Addict

At this stage he met Sundaram Gopalrao, head of a nature cure clinic in Rajmundry, who told him: "Hip baths and other kindred appliances are good as far as they go, but even they are artificial. To get rid of disease it is necessary to do away with fire in the preparation of food. We must take everything in its vital aspect as the animals do. I have cured chronic dyspepsia in old men and women through a balanced diet containing germinating seeds." This idea, propounded more than seventy years ago, is now taking root in Europe and America!

Experiments in raw food involved Gandhi in voluminous correspondence with scores who lived in the same way, and he wrote: "Dr. Ansari, who knows my body well, examined it carefully whilst I was in Delhi and was of the opinion that he had never found me in better health. My blood pressure (systolic) which after breakfast at Kolhapur had never been below 155 now registered 118; pulse pressure (beat) 46. Though 118 he thought to be normal, it was no bad sign as I had just risen from an attack of malaria and I was then living on fruit juices only."

## Gandhi and Sir Robert McCarrison, I.M.S.

He continued to experiment on himself and read Dr. Muthu's book on tuberculosis and Col. McCarrison's primer, and lived on unfired foods. At one period he ate 3½ oz sprouted wheat, 1¾ oz pounded almonds, ⅛ oz whole almonds, 7 oz green vegetables (grated), 9 oz raisins, an ounce of lemon juice, and 1½ oz honey daily. To this he later added 3½ oz coconut and 4 oz milk.

Gandhi wrote: "About nothing are we so woefully ignorant or negligent as in regard to our bodies. There are about 22 in Mandir making the experiment. Most of them have given up milk, having added bananas to their diet and increased the amount of coconut. There is no difficulty about digesting uncooked, sprouted grains, and pulses (legumes) and uncooked green vegetables."

### McCarrison's Advice

McCarrison took a keen interest in Gandhi's experiments and wrote from Coonoor in July 1929 to correct him on a number of points. He explained that one reason for the nutritive limitations of a purely vegetarian diet is the difference in the length of man's gastro-intestinal tract and that of herbivorous animals: "(a) Man's digestive tube is not long enough nor capacious enough to accommodate a sufficient mass of suitable vegetable food, nor to extract from such as it can contain all the nutriment man needs for his *fullest well-being*; (b) there is only one vitamin—vitamin D—for which man can rely (to a considerable extent) upon the sun.

"One of the great faults of Indian diets at the present day is their deficiency in vitamin A, in suitable proteins, and in certain salts; and the greatest nutritional need of India is the freer use of good milk and its products which supply these factors . . ."

Gandhi accepted McCarrison's advice with reserve and replied: "I believe . . . in the limitless vegetable kingdom there is an effective substitute for milk which, every medical man admits, has its drawbacks and is designed by nature not for man but for babies and young ones of lower animals."

By this time he had given up white sugar and taken to *gur* (molasses) and honey, and he started a correspondence with Dr. W. R. Aykroyd, Director of Nutritional Research in Coonoor, who delivered a lecture in 1935 in which he outlined details of a balanced diet for the poorest in the land costing no more than four rupees a *month* (a rupee was then equal to 1s. 6d.), which consisted of 16 oz soya beans, 2 oz *arhar dal* (lentils), 1 oz *jaggery* (molasses), 4 oz spinach, 4 oz amaranth, 1 oz potato, 1 oz colacacia, 1.5 oz coconut oil, and 6 oz buttermilk a day, the total cost of which was two annas, or less than 2½d.

In the "good old days of the Raj" the wages of the labouring classes were derisory. I was employed by the Eastern Bengal Railway, which paid its coolies 13 rupees and four annas* a month (19s. 6d.) and in comparison with coolies not in government employ these were considered well off. Food was correspondingly cheap and when I was a boy in Eastern Bengal, chickens could be bought at the rate of 22 for a rupee! Most of the people were vegetarians.

*Cheaper and Better Food*

Gandhi tried to do what Allison was doing in England; finding cheaper and better food for the millions of undernourished and, though affluent himself, existed on the cheapest and simplest fare. For example, on 22nd October, 1935, after consulting a number of medical friends he produced a balanced dinner for 98 people at a cost of 6 pice (about 1¾d.) a head—less than the sum allowed by Dr. Aykroyd. The raw materials for this banquet were: 36 lb wholemeal flour, 12 lb tomatoes, 4 lb *jaggery*, 24 lb red gourd, 6 lb linseed oil, 50 lb milk, 4 lb soya beans, 6 coconuts, and 16 *koth* fruit, together with tamarind, salt and fuel. The ingredients were made into an appetising meal which satisfied everyone.

After this he took a number of children under his wing and experimented on them, making sure they always had enough of the right kinds of food for health and growth.

Dr. Menkel, a dietitian, wrote to suggest that Indians should eat more uncooked food and vegetables and cut out

* 16 annas = 1 rupee = 1s. 6d.

sweet dishes—one of the main causes of diabetes which was so prevalent, while McCarrison suggested that fruit and berries should be taken more liberally because "they are among the best of all foodstuffs and *should form a considerable part of our daily diet.*"

## Gandhi Continued to Learn

In India the *chamars* (Untouchables) eat carrion, so Gandhi carried on a correspondence with Dr. Deshmukh to find out whether there was any difference between carrion and slaughtered meat and was informed that, scientifically speaking, there was none. "Gipsies," Deshmukh told him, "bury carcases and disinter them, and scores of persons with 'superior taste' make a point of decomposing meat before eating it; those for instance who like their grouse 'rare', or have jugged rabbit."

Deshmukh added that even when animals have been poisoned by strychnine their flesh, if eaten, will not poison humans or animals; but the idea of eating carrion or flesh of any kind revolted Gandhi.

Soon he was studying *The Newer Knowledge of Nutrition* by McCollum and Simmonds, from which he learnt more about vitamins and the value of the thin red outer skin of unpolished rice. Dr. Ansari filled gaps in his knowledge about whole-rice, *atar* (wholemeal flour) and *gur*, for McCarrison had excited his interest in wholemeal flour which he insisted was a superior article of diet to rice; so Gandhi went about urging his countrymen to substitute wholemeal flour for rice, and to ensure that if they ate rice it would be only the unpolished kind.

Next he experimented with soya beans, pulses and groundnut cake. He picked the brains of Professor Sahasrabhuhe, who had done research in ground-nuts (peanuts) and was astonished to discover how many delicious dishes could be concocted from them.

## Gandhi Learns About Vitamins

Vast tracts of India are still green and lush. McCollum's book awakened his interest in vitamins and as the villagers' diet lack these he tried to rectify the deficiency by telling people about green leaves and the vitamins they contain. While at his Wardha *ashram* (place of retreat for meditation and discussion) he experimented with *luni* and *chakwat* and the leaves of the *sarsav, suva,* turnip tops, radish tops and pea-plant leaves by pounding them, making them into pastes (*saags*) and using them as appetizers with curried vegetables. Next came the leaves of the tamarind and the *neem* (margossa), amaranth, coriander and spinach. These were pulped and made into chutnies and *saags* with the addition of a little salt, lime or lemon juice or tamarind juice. For centuries almost magical properties have been attributed to the *neem* tree.

Later he carried out investigations into vitamins, minerals and trace elements, read Dr. H. V. Tilak's book on *Balanced Diet* and in 1936 learnt that "long continued feeding of foods rich in cholesterol, vitamin D, eggs, fats (cod-liver oil and other animal fats) may produce arteriosclerosis in man." This was thirty years before the same theory was propounded by the Americans.

## Gandhi's Book

Gandhi wrote about acid-forming and alkali-forming foods in 1949 in a book entitled *Diet and Diet Reform*, published in India. He was a pioneer in growing and using soya beans though he doubted whether they were superior to the Indian lentils: *moong, udal, mussoor* and *chola.*

If an item had to be tested, he was the guinea pig; even so, to the day he was assassinated he remained fit and active. Though only a shrimp of a man—he rarely weighed as much as 100 lb—he worked harder and longer than any of his colleagues. When government officials, seekers after knowledge, and others visited his *ashram* he would show them round and, impervious to the heat, walk them off their feet. Though as thin as a bamboo with every rib in relief, he was made of old leather. "Yes", he would laugh, for he had a keen sense of humour; "not an ounce of fat. Just enough flesh to hold the bones together." On a lacto-vegetarian diet, eating only enough and no more, he was as lively as a flea.

# CHAPTER FOUR

# PLAIN, SIMPLE FOODS ARE TASTIEST

SOME of the tastiest and most nutritious dishes are made from the simplest, cheapest ingredients, such as potatoes, lentils, oats, semolina, rice, barley, wheat, eggs, cheese, nuts, yogurt and milk. Suitably combined and eaten with fruit and greens, either cooked or in salads, they provide all one needs for health.

## *The Wonderful Potato*

If potatoes cost fifty shillings a pound there would be a bigger scramble for them by exclusive *restaurateurs* than truffles. They were not eaten in Ancient India, simply because they didn't grow in the country. Potatoes are natives of Central and South America and were first mentioned by Pedro de Ceiza de Leon in 1538. The Peruvians cultivated both the common potato and the sweet potato which they called *patata*, ate it as a vegetable, made it into flour, and concocted a variety of dishes from it. To them it was what rice is to Indians and Chinese, and what wheat was to Europe. Both the French and British shunned the potato when it was first introduced; the Puritans and Scots denounced it from their pulpits as "forbidden fruit" because no mention is made of it in the Bible and, William Cobbett, who should have had more sense, said it was cattle food and the working man should not be condemned to eat it; and there sprang up a Society For The Prevention Of Unwholesome Diet, which advised people not to touch it.

Only after Marie Antoinette served the potato at court functions and wore the flowers in her hair did the French take to it; only after the British Army in Flanders were reduced either to eating the potato or starving in 1914, did they realize how good it was; but in Ireland it was adopted with enthusiasm and priests and altar boys went about sprinkling the fields with holy water as an inducement to farmers to cultivate the potato. Once established, the potato never looked back.

## Potatoes Are Not Fattening

The potato is not a perfect food. No food is. But it is as near a perfect food as any comestible. Potatoes vary in their composition but within limits consist of 68-80 per cent water, 0.69-.067 per cent protein, 16-19 per cent carbohydrate (starch), 0.4-0.96 per cent fat, 0.28-3.48 per cent fibre, 0.53-1.87 per cent mineral salts, and a potato baked in its jacket contains 130 units of vitamin A, 130 units of vitamin B, and 20-75 units of vitamin C per pound; so it is a fairly good source of all three.

Because of its large water content it is NOT fattening but—here lies the snag—as it can absorb one fifth of its weight in fat without tasting oily and as fried potatoes are delectable, most people eat them that way and put on pounds. Fat is the culprit, not the potato. Incidentally, don't boil potatoes to death because excessive boiling kills the vitamin C.

## Good Protein

Though the potato is *not* a protein food, the protein part, called tuberin, contains 60-70 per cent nitrogenous matter and controlled experiments have shown that it will sustain life over long periods even if no other form of protein is eaten.  M. S. Rose existed for four years on a diet consisting of potatoes and milk, and a number of experimenters have lived for up to 300 days on potatoes and a little fat.

Dr. M. Hindhede, Director of the State Laboratory for Food Research, Copenhagen, wrote: "The nourishment that we take and the composition and preparation of our food are all factors of the greatest importance to the health of the individual and his physical and mental efficiency." During the First World War he was invited by his government to work out a plan for feeding the people effectively.

"To state the matter bluntly," he wrote, "the people were fed on animal fodder. They were given plenty of potatoes and substantial bread in the form of whole-meal rye bread in which the full natural content of starch had been increased by a further 15 per cent of bran; besides this, plenty of oatmeal and potatoes, some milk, butter and vegetables, but little meat." Only the rich could afford what little meat there was.

"This eminently vegetarian diet, which rather lacked albuminoids, agreed with my countrymen. Their health improved and the death rate fell considerably (to the lowest ever in Europe!). I tested this diet in the State physiological food laboratory during many years with many foodstuffs on a number of people following different occupations. I wish to emphasise that this system of nourishment does *not* produce weakness or tiredness, but on the contrary, increases efficiency and joy of living."

## Getting the Best Out of The Potato

Chips and crisps are well known standbys; most people eat roast-potatoes with the Sunday joint, and when new and succulent the potato is boiled and eaten with peas and mint sauce; but comparatively few eat the potato baked in its jacket—which is the best way.

Take one or two large floury potatoes—the waxy varieties are unsuitable—scrub them thoroughly with a stiff brush under flowing water, then dry and prick all over with a fork or the tip of a sharp knife. Smear them with very little butter, margarine or olive oil and pop them into the oven at 300 degrees Fah. (gas No. 6) and within an hour or an hour and a half they should be cooked through. The fat on the skins keeps them tender so that the entire potato can be relished.

Cut them in half, scoop a little out of the middles and pop in butter, or some other fat, finely chopped herbs, and a shake of pepper and a *little* salt. Eaten like this with salad, or on their own, they're delicious.

Alternatively, chop two cloves of garlic finely (or chives) and mix this into the butter. This gives the potato an unusual piquancy and turns it into a relish. If you use raw garlic, however, make sure that you're not visiting friends, though by chewing raw parsley the taint of garlic on the breath can be nullified. Incidentally, I don't sprinkle salt on potatoes, eggs, salads or other foods, though lentils are tasteless to most people without salt.

## Soup

If most people want soup they open a can and add either milk or water to the contents, or add gravy in the form of hot water mixed with Oxo, Bovril, Marmite, Beetox or other flavouring. To me that isn't soup, despite what the TV adverts say; it's an insult. The adverts tell us that women put on evening dress and men dinner jackets, sit at shining mahogany tables laid with priceless silver and eat baked beans and canned peas in the romantic glow of candle light. One wonders who the advertisers are conning; is anyone with a brain larger than a peanut taken in?

## Onion and Potato Soup

Tasty and nutritious soups do not take long to make. Take two large potatoes and boil them briskly till soft. Drain the water into a bowl and mash the potatoes roughly with a fork.

Slice two large onions finely. Fry them in a little butter or other fat till brown, drain off the fat and fry a couple of stale slices of wholemeal bread in the fat. Then cut the bread into cubes.

Put the onions and mashed potato into the onion water, bring to the boil, then simmer for a minute or two and serve with the cubes of fried bread floating in it. A sprinkle of pepper and a *little* salt may be added, and chopped parsley will improve the flavour.

When the bread is being fried, chopped garlic may be added to the fat, which gives it a distinctive flavour (it will not affect the breath). Alternatively, grated cheese may be sprinkled on the bread as it floats on the soup; or ground paprika. There isn't only one way to serve any dish; ingenuity and imagination lend variety.

### The Much Ignored Lentil

People look down their noses at lentils as food for the poor. "Pease pudding", they sneer, "good enough for Oliver Twist in the workhouse. All very well for the Scots or Northcountry folk." But lentils are not merely cheap; they're extremely nutritious and can be very tasty. They consist of 12.35 per cent water, 25.70 per cent protein (steak is only 18 per cent), 1.9 per cent fat, 53.30 per cent carbohydrate, and 3.04 per cent mineral matter.

A thick lentil soup, a couple of slices of wholemeal bread, a little fresh fruit, or stewed fruit and cream, make a substantial meal.

### Lentil Soup

Bring two or three pints of water *to the boil* and pour in a breakfast cup of lentils. If the water is not boiling the lentils will not break up easily. After a minute, turn down the heat till the water just bubbles. In half an hour the lentils will be soft. Remove the pan from the stove and whisk the mixture till the lentils are broken and the liquid thick. Add a *little* salt.

Chop a couple of medium-size onions finely and fry them in a little fat till brown. Drain off the fat. Bring the lentils to the boil again, slip in the browned onions, simmer for a minute, mix well and serve with parsley or other garnishing. Eat with brown bread.

### Lentil Loaf

One cup lentils, 1 cup breadcrumbs, 1 cup nut milk, 1 tablespoon chopped parsley, ½ teaspoon sage, salt to taste.

Cover the lentils in boiling water and soak overnight. Then mix the ingredients well, place in a greased pan and bake in a moderate oven till firm. An egg or even two may be mixed with the ingredients, but this is optional.

### Lentil and Potato Loaf

Two cups lentils; 2 cups boiled potatoes, chopped; 3 tablespoons nut cream; ½ teaspoon sage, 1 tablespoon chopped parsley; 1 or 2 eggs; 1 tablespoon melted butter; salt to taste.

Cover lentils in boiling water and stand overnight. Mix lentils, nut cream and sage and put into a greased dish. Cover with potato, brush with melted butter and bake till light brown. Serve with parsley. Beans may be used in place of lentils.

### Lentil Savouries

In India, where wonders are worked with lentils, they make excellent savouries with them, which may either form a meal, or top one off. One kind, known as *bhajias*, are made from lentil flour which may be bought from any shop selling Indian spices. The flour is known as *basoon* (pronounced *bay-soon*).

### Bhajias or Spiced Vegetable Savoury Balls

Four tablespoons *basoon;* ½ teaspoon chilli powder; 2 teaspoons ground cummin; 1 medium size onion, chopped; 1 teaspoon ground coriander; 2 cloves garlic, chopped; salt to taste.

Melt a pound of butter, margarine or cooking fat in a chip pan. Make a pancake type batter with the *basoon* and cold water. Mix in salt, spices, galic and onion.

Bring the fat to the boil, take a teaspoonful of the batter and drop it gently into the fat where it will instantly bubble and sizzle. Cook till the outside of the batter is light brown, then remove and drain. This should take about half a minute. In a large pan six or seven spoons of batter can be cooked at the same time.

Diced vegetables such as cooked potato, carrot, beet, parsnip, or raw chopped cabbage may be mixed into the batter; or small quantities of cold meat chopped into little pieces. An excellent way to finish left-overs.

If the batter is mixed and allowed to stand, the *bhajias* can be made quickly when you return on a winter's night and make an excellent supper dish; but if made and left, are liable to turn leathery. The chilli, which lends pungency, can be left out altogether, or added to.

# CHAPTER FIVE

# WHY IGNORE HERBS?

IN India herbs—cooked and raw—are more widely eaten than in any country in the world. Curry ingredients consist either of herbs or the spices of herbal plants. All are antiseptic because in the tropics food will not keep for more than a few hours when cooked before chemical changes and putrefaction sets in. This applies particularly to fish, flesh and fowl, which herb spices preserve. If every householder in Britain with a garden reserved a patch for herbs and used them regularly, cooked and raw, there would be less need for visits to the doctor. In May, before the early lettuces have made their appearance, there are chives, marjoram, mint and sage and within a few weeks land cress (the seed of which can be bought), and parsley. Land cress can be cut and eaten from June to October, when water cress is no longer available. In India a pungent member of the cress family is chopped and eaten raw, mixed with oil, vinegar and tomato.

## Curry Herbs

Most readers will be surprised to learn that Indian curries which look and taste so different from English fare, contain in varying quantities such spices as aniseed, allspice, cardamom, mace, nutmeg, cinnamon, coriander, cummin, cloves, black pepper, mustard seed, chillis, turmeric, saffron, fenugreek, garlic, ginger (dry and green), poppy seed, asafoetida, almond and coconut. Except coriander and cummin, all these are well known to British housewives.

## Spices Are Medicinal

Spices aren't "messed about" in any way and they are nature's medicaments. Chilli belongs to the paprika family and is one of the richest in vitamin C. Ginger has long been used in the East and is mentioned in Chinese medicinal books, in Sanskrit literature and in the Talmud. Ginger cordial is excellent for keeping out the cold, especially if served with a splash of brandy, whisky or rum.

Turmeric, used widely in the East for healing bruises and for leech-bites, is a carminative.

Garlic and onion are among the finest herbs on earth; cinnamon and cloves are powerful germicides. Some years ago the scientist Cavel infected some beef-tea with water taken from a sewage system and added to one sample oil of cinnamon diluted to 4 parts in 1,000, and oil of cloves diluted to 2 parts in 1,000 to another. In each the germs were utterly destroyed; but carbolic acid in a strength of 5.6 parts in 1,000 had to be used before germs in a third sample were destroyed. Yet how many people realize that the oils of cinnamon and cloves are more powerful antiseptics than carbolic acid; and of course, more palatable.

Coriander is a carminative and an antiseptic; in the Middle Ages cordials were made from it, the best known being the famous *Eau de Carmes* prepared by the Carmelite monks from lemon peel, coriander, nutmeg, cloves, cinnamon, angelica roots and spirits of wine.

Both nutmeg and mace contain valuable oils used in cases of renal and hepatic colic and for nervous maladies. Nutmeg oil aids digestion, is a carminative and is given for dysentry, and to counteract the effect of certain poisons. In the East it is applied to the temples to induce sleep and nutmeg tea is an Old English cure for insomnia. Mace is well known in English cookery.

## The Value of Peppers

Peppers have always been looked at askance by food reformers because they are supposed to irritate the lining of the stomach; but any food or herb eaten to excess is harmful in some way. A *little* pepper lends piquancy to food; not enough to stimulate, for good food needs no stimulation. Black pepper is often administered in the East for fever, in doses of six to ten grains in the form of pills because, unlike quinine it does not suppress, but raises temperature, causes intense sweating, gets rid of toxins, and burns out fever. Allspice falls into the same category. Peppers are rich in vitamin C.

Mustard is also used in curries; the seed for flavouring and the oil for cooking. According to *Diet and Diet Reform** it contains from 98-99 per cent fat, with traces of manganese, nickel and cobalt and if the skin, which contains ergosterol, is rubbed with mustard oil and exposed to the sun, the sunlight is converted into vitamin D. Since time immemorial mustard oil has formed the base of many unguents and embrocations and Pliny wrote: "It is so pungent in flavour that it burns like fire, though at the same time it is remarkably wholesome for the body."

Aniseed and fennel are both used in curries and in Old England the first was eaten to promote appetite and still forms the base of cough mixtures and lozenges. The second was so highly esteemed by the Welsh that they had a saying: "He who sees fennel and gathers it not, is not a man but a devil." It is widely used in Mediterranean cuisine, is excellent in fish sauces and dressings, and the seeds add flavour to pastry. The French use dried fennel stalks for flaming *loup de mer* and as an aromatic in *bouillabaise*; the Italians use the bulbs of fresh fennel mixed with lemon and oil, for salad dressing. Gradually it is growing popular in Britain once more.

*Cardamoms*

In Britain the cardamom is almost unknown, except to those versed in Indian cookery. The oil is powerfully

* M. K. Gandhi

antiseptic and is used in the manufacture of some perfumes. The Germans are the biggest buyers in Europe. The seeds, either whole or ground, are used in curries and in sweets, particularly in delicious rice puddings called *kheer*. They make a world of difference to ordinary rice pudding.

Indians have also for centuries used poppy seed, which is extremely popular among Slavs; fenugreek, bay leaves, asafoetida, lemon grass, and the juices of the lime, lemon and tamarind.

## The Blessings of Immigration

Immigration is not the unadulterated curse that some would have us believe, for successive waves of immigrants have made the British what they are. Their ways, customs, habits, food, industries and outlook have been assimilated into our culture and enriched it. Without the influx of the Dutch there would have been no bulb industry and Lincolnshire would indeed be drab without her thousands of acres of tulips. The Huguenots taught us about spinning and fine textiles and gave Britain a new industry; the French introduced us to the salad as we know it today and taught us much about good cooking; the Belgians and Danes introduced the art of pastry making: they and the French brought in fine cheeses; even the barbarous, hairy-kneed Scots taught the untutored English how to make porridge, bannocks, griddle cakes, baps and scones, and introduced them to the mysteries of the bagpipes and haggis. In Britain today there are thousands of immigrants from the East and the West Indies, all eating exotic foods which the more courageous of us sample and grow to like. They lend variety to our diet and provide food elements not easily obtained. Unfortunately people in Britain don't associate curried foods with health because of the excessive amounts of chilli that Indian and Pakistani *restaurateurs* put into their dishes because most Britons imagine a curry is no good unless it burns a hole in the roof of one's mouth. In actual fact, anyone who knows will tell you that the best curries are extremely mild and delicately flavoured. The only fire-eaters are Englishmen out East, who don't know better.

### Are Herbs Weeds?

Herbs abound in English gardens, though most gardeners, who don't realize their value, dig them out and burn them. In doing so they discard valuable health-giving foods.

What is a weed? The dictionary definition is: "a herbaceous plant not valued for use or beauty, growing wild and *rank*, and regarded as encumbering the ground or hindering the growth of *superior* vegetation." It goes on to explain that among other things, *rank* means "vigorous and luxuriant in growth." Which is just what weeds are. The nettles at the bottom of my garden, which are boiled and eaten every spring, are certainly vigorous and luxuriant; the tender tops taste like spinach and at a time when few other greens can be had are delicious with poached eggs on top, or made into spinach pasties with potatoes, beans, cauliflower and nut-meat. The water in which they are boiled makes fine soup stock. Nettles are good for skin diseases and were eaten by our forefathers to purify the blood each spring. Nature put them into the soil for a very good reason, but because they grow in profusion, overwhelm less robust plants and cost nothing, they are scorned. Years ago when I had an attack of lumbago I got my wife, much against her better judgment, to apply stinging nettles to my back, which cured me instantly and, believe it or not, the treatment was painless!

John Parkinson, the King's Herbalist, wrote in 1640 that Roman soldiers used nettles "to rubbe and chafe their limbs, when through extreme cold they should be stiffe and benummed." The nettle is not a native of Britain but was brought over by the Romans and is one of the many blessings we owe to them. It cures rheumatism by the formic acid which is injected through hollow tubes in the hairs, and causes inflammation and the drawing out of poisons through the skin. And now that home-made wines have become popular, we are realizing what a pleasant, health-giving drink nettle beer is.

## Eat Your Weeds

Some of the waste in kitchen scrap bins could well be eaten with benefit to health. Most people who pull up raw beets cut off the stalks and leaves and throw them away. They'd be surprised to learn that in America doctors now recommend beet leaves for the cure of arthritis.

In our abysmal ignorance we throw away many health-giving herbs. Young dandelion leaves which impart a pleasantly bitter flavour to salads; young nasturtium leaves which give them a pungent tang; chopped marigolds can be put into stews and salads, floated on soups or porridge, added to cordials and, if pounded with sugar, can be made into conserves that are good for invalids. The flowers, if rubbed into the skin, relieve bee stings; and wine can be brewed from either the whole flowers or the petals alone. The same applies to the dandelion, rose, elder-flower and a host of others. Every part of the elder, from the root to the flower has health-giving properties.

## Garden Herbs

So many excellent herbs grow wild in our woods, fields and hedges that it would need a thick book to tell you about them and their excellent properties. Even those grown in gardens are not made full use of; mint, sage, thyme, basil, marjoram (origano), rosemary, chervil, chives, parsley, and tarragon, to name a few. Let me tell you about them.

*Sage*
Bitter, fragrant and strong. A little goes a long way in soups, salads, mixed into stuffing and pasties.

*Thyme*
Pungent and aromatic; can be used in stews and soups.

*Marjoram*
Also pungent; excellent for soups, stews, sauces and stuffing.

*Parsley*
Normally used only as an adjunct to fish, either as sauce or garnishing, but it can be used in almost any dish.

*Tarragon*
A superb flavouring. Chopped finely and mixed with melted butter, makes a splendid sauce. Try it in scrambled egg; in omelette; in soups.

*Chives*
Used chopped, in salads; as garnish; in dressings of every kind, cooked or raw.

*Mint*
The unimaginative can think of nothing in connection with mint other than sauce. Mint, chives, parsley and marjoram, either singly or mixed and chopped finely, go well when sprinkled on soups; and mixed with butter, cream cheese, peanut butter or other paste, make tasty sandwich fillings. Mint forms the basis of mint julep, a refreshing hot weather drink.

Incidentally, a handful of parsley steeped in boiling water for 15 minutes and taken by the wineglassful four or five times a day, relieves bladder troubles and cystitis rapidly.

*Sandwiches For Health*
Little did the Earl of Sandwich realize, when he refused

to be lured from the card table and subsisted on slices of bread with meat between them, what he had started. Not only is the sandwich the most convenient form of food for the traveller, but it is capable of immense variation and can form a delicious meal. The Danes, who have brought sandwich making to an art, produce more than 200 kinds, some two- and three-decker sandwiches with fillings of every sort, though apparently British cafes restrict theirs to meat, cheese and tomato, with or without mustard. Few people have a greater ability for making good ingredients more unappetizing.

## The Sandwich Lunch

Don't scorn the sandwich lunch. It can be worth making. Women in particular, would rather take sandwiches for lunch than undergo the ordeal of a heavy meal at mid-day. All one needs to make sandwiches appetizing, is imagination. Here are a few elementary rules: (1) Never make sandwiches of new bread; (2) they are better if the bread is a day old, and firm; (3) always use genuine wholemeal bread; unless it can't be obtained, don't be put off with anything less; (4) cut the slices thinly. Doorsteps may look sustaining but you're eating more bread than filling, and it's the filling that gives flavour and sustains. All bread and little filling is fattening. You can eat far more thin sandwiches with plenty of filling than thick slices with little filling.

## An Endless Variety of Fillings

(1) Cream cheese, cottage cheese or curd cheese; or cheese that has been kept and hardened. Grate it finely; don't be miserly; use plenty. Pop into the garden and pluck a handful or two of herbs: mint, parsley, marjoram, chives, thyme, or just one or two kinds. (2) Wash and chop them finely. (3) Add to the cheese and mix thoroughly with a fork. (4) Smear this thickly on each slice of the sandwich,

not merely on one slice. This makes a great difference to the taste. (5) Make more sandwiches than you need because if you offer them round, your friends are bound to come back for more. (6) Put them in a polythene container with a tightly fitting lid and pop them into the fridge and they'll be fresh when you take them out at lunch time next day. Three or four sandwiches followed by a banana, apple or pear and washed down by tea, milk, coffee, fruit juice or plain water, make a sustaining meal.

The flavours may be varied by using Marmite, Beetox, or other flavouring; or instead of cheese use peanut butter, hazelnut, almond, or walnut butter, chopped and mashed figs, raisins or dates, or one of the many nut creams sold in health food shops.

You needn't have all the sandwiches of the same kind; one may have cheese and parsley, another peanut butter and mint, a third grated cheese and a mixture of herbs; fillings of tomato, cucumber or anything else you wish.

Friends who visit us for tea say invariably that they've never tasted such sandwiches before and had no idea that such fillings could be so tasty. You may add all sorts of other flavours; dandelion and nasturtium leaves, a touch of India lime pickle or mango chutney—anything that lends variety. Why not? Just because it's never been done before, there's no reason for not trying it. There's a first time for everything.

*Nut and Dried Fruit Sandwiches*

Imagination plays an important part in food; it makes the difference between a cook and a chef. Try fruit and nut sandwiches. (1) Put seedless raisins through a mincer or grinder, or chop them into little pieces with a sharp knife. (2) Add a little butter or cream cheese and mash well with a fork till thoroughly mixed. (3) Smear the paste thickly on each slice of the sandwich. (4) You may add milled nuts to the mixture, with a spoonful of thick honey. You can do this with apricots and other dried fruit, such as dried bananas. Use any filling you can think of; sandwiches need not be made of mousetrap cheese and wilting lettuce.

You can make similar sandwiches if you're having people in for tea; put them in the fridge in air-tight polythene boxes and they'll keep fresh for 24 hours if need be.

## Sandwiches Are Meals

Don't regard sandwiches as a stop-gap till you can have a meal. They are real, nourishing meals. Use the best ingredients and take trouble in making them. Always apply the filling generously, and to both slices—and cut the bread thinly. You want to taste the filling; not merely the bread, though good wholemeal bread, such as you buy at Cranks, at Health Food Stores, or at Selfridges, is tasty enough to be eaten and relished without any filling. Fillings make such bread even more delectable.

# CHAPTER SIX

# LIVING WITHOUT ANIMAL PRODUCTS

THOUGH it is possible to live healthily without animal products, even milk, cheese and eggs, those who intend to do so should first learn something about dietetics, otherwise their diet will probably be unbalanced and they may fall ill. The idea, however, that either a vegetarian diet, or Food Reform, is dull and tasteless, is nonsense as anyone who visits places like Cranks or The Vega, or stays in one of the vegetarian country houses that cater for vegetarians, knows.

## No Roast Meat and Two-Veg

Most meat-eaters on holiday croon with delight if served with roast meat and two-veg., with steamed pudding or fruit salad from a can, topped with ice cream, an unimaginative diet which follows them about like a hound with his nose to a bag of aniseed.

Vegetarian houses that served a similar monotonous diet day after day would soon go out of business; they have to use imagination, so make jellies from seaweed, flavoured with lemon, vanilla and fruit juices, exotic salads, nut roasts and delicious vegetable pies.

## The Soya Bean

The soya bean has been eaten in China for thousands of years and has given the Chinese worker amazing stamina and a tough physique. It is richer in protein than any food, including flesh and fish, and has an alkaline reaction. One ounce of lean mutton contains 5.97 grammes of protein, fish 5.50, chicken 6.74, egg 3.79, wheat, 3.90, soya bean 9.60, and the calories in these foods are 43, 32, 30, 42, 28 and 119 respectively. The soya bean scores all along the line.

Major-General Sir Robert McCarrison said that if only Indians could be induced to make the soya bean their national food all their nutritional problems would vanish; and Dr. McCollum of Johns Hopkins University maintained that if Americans tempered their diet with soya beans there would be a drop of at least 20 per cent in their mortality rate. The soya bean is particularly suited to the middle-aged and old because it prevents hardening of the arteries and premature senility.

### Rich In Vitamin C

In parts of North China where the winter has a Siberian intensity and fresh vegetables are scarce, soya beans take their place. A Chinese family will cover a quart of beans in water for 24 hours, then strain and place a weighted board on top to press them down and stow them in the warmest corner of the kitchen. Soon the beans sprout and when the sprouts are half an inch long, or longer they are ready to be eaten.

A pan of water is brought to the boil, the heat turned off and the beans put in. When cool, as many beans as are needed are taken out and shelled. The sprouts are soaked for ten minutes, oil, vinegar and chopped onion are added and they are served, either hot or cold, with meat, fish, bean curd or vegetables.

### Bean Curd

Bean curd is easy to make, very nutritious, and can be eaten in many ways: sweet, savoury, or flavoured. Take a quart of yellow beans (or less), add water and grind them into a paste, or put them through a coffee mill and make them into a paste with water. Put the paste into a pan, cover with water and boil for an hour; then add gelatine made from seaweed.

Strain the water, put the curd into a cheese cloth and press between two boards or place a weight on it as if making cottage cheese. When thoroughly drained, cut into large squares. It is now ready for use.

Take one of the large squares, cut into half-inch cubes, soak in hot water for ten minutes, fry in oil or fat with onions and garlic, and eat with chopped herbs.

If a sweet is wanted, mix sugar or honey with the paste, and add flavouring such as vanilla, lime, etc.

## Nuts Are Good Foods

In comedies and music-hall sketches, mothers-in-law and vegetarians are always good for a laugh. "Jenkins is a vegetarian," says the comedian; "he's coming for lunch—what shall we give him to eat?"

"A raw carrot, a handful of nuts and a lettuce leaf," replies the stooge. It invariably brings the house down.

Nuts are not considered as food. They're all right to crack while the port is going round, to munch while hiking or at a football match, to fill the empty spaces between lunch and tea, or to crack on a winter's night and toss the shells on the fire. But humans can't *live* on nuts. They're not monkeys.

## Nuts Give Gorillas Their Strength

Our closest relatives, the anthropoids, thrive on nuts. A chimpanzee can shift half a ton as easily as a porter handles your suitcase and gorillas have been known to bend sporting rifles in their hands like pieces of wire, so there is little reason to assume that nuts give them strength, but not us.

## Edible Nuts

In Britain the walnut, peanut, Brazil, hazel nut and the almond are common. The chestnut is seldom regarded as a nut; it is eaten as a vegetable and used for stuffing; the acorn is scorned as food fit only for pigs, though in Spain and in parts of Turkey sweets and savouries are made from it. There are more than a score of nuts, ranging from pine kernels to pistachios that can be eaten and enjoyed.*

Nuts are rich in phosphoric acid, potash and magnesium and all nuts are easily digested if only you will take the trouble to chew them into a paste before swallowing. Their digestibility is increased if eaten in combination with raw leafy vegetables, or fruit, or both. Nuts should not be eaten in large quantities or as dessert after a heavy meal because they need the full action of the digestive juices. Eaten with leafy vegetables and fresh fruit they form a well balanced meal.

*Miscellaneous Publication No. 572*

In its *Miscellaneous Publication No. 572* the U.S. Department of Agriculture stated that legumes and nuts excel whole-grain cereals as sources of calcium and are rich in iron; and both rank above whole-grain cereals as sources of calcium.

Sir Frederick Gowland Hopkins, who put vitamins on the map, said that in the field of foods and nutrition, tradition tends to accumulate prejudices as well as truths. How right he was! For years we have had it drummed into us that animal protein is first class and vegetable protein second class. "This we know from modern research," writes Henry C. Sherman, Mitchell Professor of Chemistry, Columbia University, one of the foremost nutritionists in the world, "to be an unsound generalization, yet this prejudiced and prejudicial inheritance from a pre-scientific yesterday persists; and one often meets the term 'animal protein' used as a part of a dietary description or specification in a way that plainly perpetuates the fallacy.

"Chemical research on the amino-acid constitution of

* *About Nuts and Dried Fruit*

animal proteins and nutritional research with human subjects in balance experiments and with laboratory experiments over long segments of the life-cycle (including periods of rapid growth) rank the proteins of soya beans and peanuts with animal proteins in chemical nature and nutritional efficiency; and show further that the proteins of our ordinary beans and peas need little supplementation in order to nourish us equally well. Thus clearly, the soybean crop of the United States constitutes a very large potential source for improved human nutrition."

He adds: "The use as human food of whole peanuts or peanut butter is also worthy of fuller appreciation and further development. The eating of roasted whole peanuts, either alone or with fruits or sweets, is nutritionally an excellent food habit and is also exceedingly convenient.

"Roasted peanuts ground to peanut butter also make a highly nutritious and convenient food. In a sandwich peanut butter fills the place of both butter and meat."*

## Digestibility of Nut Butters

Investigation carried out at Yale University have shown that nuts contain a relatively high amount of basic amino acids; that their proteins have a high biological value and are adequate to maintain life and growth. In tests conducted at the Sheffield Laboratory, Professor Cajori found that the proteins and fats of nuts were nearly all absorbed, especially when nuts were eaten in the form of nut butters. This is important in an age when so many have to resort to dentures after the age of thirty and find it difficult to grind nuts sufficiently for assimilation.

Nuts must be ground to a paste, for even the smallest particles cannot be easily penetrated and acted on by digestive juices and enzymes, and so pass undigested into the alimentary canal. Digestibility is increased by more than

* *Foods: Their Values and Management*

ten per cent if nuts are eaten in the form of nut butters, which are sold in all health-food shops.

## Salted Nuts

The belief that salted nuts *prevent* digestive troubles associated with such food, is unfounded. In fact, *salt interferes with the digestion* not only of nuts, but all foods. Nuts ground in a mill and sprinkled on salads, vegetables and fruit, lend variety to meals, and children should be encouraged to eat fruit—cooked or raw—in this way rather than sweets made with sugar or glucose. Nuts ground and mixed into cakes, make them far more nourishing and tasty.

## Madeira Cake

A thick slice of Madeira cake and a glass of milk will make a sustaining lunch if you're in a hurry. Ingredients consist of: 8 oz 100 per cent wholemeal self-raising flour; 8 oz Barbadoes sugar; 8 oz butter; 2 oz milled almonds; the rind of two lemons. Mix all the ingredients thoroughly and add two eggs, also well mixed. Place in a greased baking tin, cover with grease-proof paper and bake in a pre-heated oven for half an hour at 400 degrees Fah., and then for an hour at 200 degrees Fah., reducing the heat gradually. Don't buy ground almonds because you don't know how long they've been kept. Mill the almonds in their brown skins and the taste will be much improved.

You can also make your own marzipan with either honey and milled nuts, or Barbadoes sugar and milled nuts. It will taste better than the stuff you can buy.

## Digestibility of Nuts

Except for the chestnut, chufa-nut and coconut, nuts as a whole contain little carbohydrate and their fat, which helps to keep out the cold, is much more easily digested than animal fats. They are a good substitute for those with whom milk fats don't agree. Animal fats are free fats and will not mix with water, whereas nut-fats do, and can be emulsified into cream.

Fats are easily digested when one has an ample supply of organic sodium in food, for sodium is the principal alkaline element in the process of saponification carried on by the pancreatic juice, bile and intestinal juice. In order to function efficiently intestinal juice needs carbonate of soda, which not only neutralizes acids in the intestinal tract but emulsifies the fats.

The digestion of nuts, therefore, will always be helped by eating plenty of fruit and vegetables which are rich in sodium, but not by the addition of *inorganic* salt (table salt). When nuts are roasted and salted the proteins coagulate, the fats split into glycerine and free fatty acids, and the vitamins are impaired, if not destroyed.

## Nut Butter

Nut butter can be bought in half-pound packets or made at home. If the nuts are moist they will clog your mill, so place them in an oven and heat them slightly, but do not roast. Don't blanch almonds or rub the red skins off peanuts because these contain valuable nutrients, in the case of peanuts, aneurin. Large nuts should be broken in smaller pieces for easy grinding. When milled they can be mashed into a smooth butter.

Coconut can be shredded, granulated, desiccated, and then mashed; or made into coconut milk, which gives added flavour to soups, stews, casserole dishes and makes the world of difference to a curry.

## Coconut Milk

Beat one cup of grated coconut with two cups of boiling water for ten minutes; then let the mixture stand for an hour, after which the liquid should be strained through a cheese cloth. After the milk has been extracted the flesh may be soaked in two cups of boiling water for a second time and allowed to stand for two or three hours, or over-night, after which a second extraction may be obtained. This will be weaker than the first extraction. The flesh can be fed to chickens or put on the compost heap.

## Combination Nut Butter

Grind equal parts of peanuts, pignolias and grated coconut, mash and mix into a paste. You can do this with any combination of nuts and vary the taste to your liking.

## Nut Cream

This may be bought in health-food stores but is just as good and much cheaper if made at home. To make nut cream, dissolve some nut butter in warm water, mixing and adding water gradually to get the amount and thickness you desire. Some of these creams—coconut, almond and Brazil—may be used in place of dairy cream, and the addition of honey improves the flavour. Other pleasant flavours are vanilla, made with a vanilla pod, and mint, made with the finely chopped and mashed herb. Make only the amount of nut cream you need because it's always best when fresh. Two tablespoons of nut butter will make one cup of cream.

## Nut Milk

To make nut milk, add water to nut cream till it's the right consistency. With the addition of honey it goes well with fruit; the best kind, especially for children, is nut milk made from almonds, as it is alkalinising. Nut milk should be sipped slowly; never gulped.

Nuts lend themselves to all sorts of delicious concoctions and it is possible even to make custard with them.

### Nut Cream Custard

For this you need three eggs, a dessertspoon of honey, two breakfast cups of nut milk and flavouring—lemon, lime, mint, vanilla, chocolate, etc.

Beat the eggs, add honey and flavouring, then the nut cream, and whisk. Pour into custard dishes and steam or bake. Remove from the oven when an inserted knife comes out clean. Don't cook till the custard is hard and bubbly.

For thin custard to be poured over fruit, beat the egg whites stiff, then add nut cream and yolks, cook and stir continually. Take the pan off the heat the moment the custard adheres to the spoon.

Now for some nut recipes.

### Savoury Nut Loaf

If you've never tried a nut loaf, do so and discover how good it can be.

One cup ground cereals or bread crumbs; 3 cups finely chopped vegetables; 6 cloves garlic, chopped finely; 2 cups thin nut butter dressing; 1 tablespoon savoury herbs, chopped (marjoram, chives, sage, etc.); 1 tablespoon chopped parsley.

Mix well, put into a greased dish and bake for 45 minutes at 350 degrees Fah. or No. 6 (gas).

### Spinach Nut Loaf.

One cup pignolias or peanuts, finely ground; 1 bunch spinach, well washed and chopped; 1 large onion, finely chopped; 3 cloves garlic, chopped; 2 tablespoons chopped parsley; 1 cup wholemeal breadcrumbs; 3 eggs, well beaten.

Steam the spinach till tender, then add nuts, eggs, breadcrumbs, garlic, and onion and mix thoroughly. Shape into a loaf or put into an oval greased dish, brush with butter or vegetable oil, and bake in a moderate oven for an hour. In the spring an equal quantity of nettle leaves may be used instead of spinach. The flavour will be rather more bitter, but excellent.

### Peanut Loaf

Two cups peanuts; 2 cups wholemeal bread crumbs or flaked cereals; 1 cup water of tomato juice (or puree); 3 eggs, well beaten; 1 large onion, chopped; 6 cloves garlic, chopped; 2 tablespoons self-raising wholemeal flour.

Mix the ingredients thoroughly and bake in a moderate oven for about an hour.

### Nut and Rice Loaf

One cup nut meal (almonds or filberts); 2 cups boiled whole rice; 1 cup nut milk. Mix the ingredients and press into a greased pan and bake in a moderate oven for half an hour.

### Walnut Patties

One cup ground walnuts; 2 cups finely ground wholemeal breadcrumbs; 1 large grated carrot; 1 large finely chopped onion; 6 cloves garlic, chopped; 3 eggs, well beaten; 2 cups tomato juice or strained pulp.

Mix thoroughly the walnuts, crumbs, carrot, onion and garlic; fold in the eggs and mix again. Shape into patties, put into a large dish, cover with tomato and bake in a moderate oven for 25 minutes.

### Nut and Banana Loaf

Half lb almonds, finely ground; $\frac{1}{2}$ cup flaked whole wheat; 2 ripe bananas finely mashed; 1 cup chopped seedless raisins; $\frac{1}{2}$ cup water. Optional, 2 eggs, well beaten.

Mix the ingredients well, put into a greased pan and bake in a moderate oven for 45 minutes.

### Nut Cheese

One cup peanut butter; 1 cup whole corn meal, finely

ground; 2½ cups warm water; 1 teaspoon mixed herbs, chopped; 1 teaspoon parsley.

Steam the corn meal in half a cup of water for an hour. Make the cream of the nut butter and one cup of water. Add herbs and corn meal and cook for half an hour. When cold the mixture can be sliced like cheese.

### Nut Oatmeal

Two cups oatmeal; 1 cup unroasted peanut butter; 3 cups warm water; 1 teaspoon salt—or less (optional).

Steam the oatmeal with two cups of water for an hour. Mix the peanut butter with one cup of water to the consistency of cream, stir into the oatmeal and cook for another hour.

### Almond and Vegetable Roast

Two cups diced potatoes; 1 large partly cooked carrot; 1 cup sliced onion, lightly browned; 1 tablespoon fresh garden herbs; 1 cup tender new peas; 1 cup wholemeal breadcrumbs; 3 eggs, well beaten; 1 cup tomato puree; 6 cloves garlic, chopped.

Chop the herbs well, mix with the tomato and simmer for ten minutes. When cool, stir in eggs and any seasoning you wish to add; then mix potato, carrot, peas, crumbs, fried onions and garlic with the herbs and tomato, spoon into a buttered dish about two inches deep and bake in a moderate oven for an hour. Serve with gravy, potatoes, greens or salad.

*Note:* Chopped garlic has been added to most of the recipes because nothing makes such dishes as garlic. If you don't like garlic, leave it out; but garlic is the Queen of Herbs.* Salt may be added to any recipe in the quantity you desire.

As yoga is an Indian philosophy and curries Indian fare, you may care to try one. All the ingredients may be had at

* *Whole Foods for Health*

stores selling Indian spices; at Selfridges, Harrods, many Boots chemist shops, and from big food shops.

Ingredients: 4 small aubergenes; 4 cloves garlic; 4 medium size potatoes; $\frac{1}{2}$ lb carrots; 4 large onions; 1-lb can of tomatoes; $\frac{1}{2}$ lb broad beans or peas; 3 red chillis (optional); 2 teaspoons ground coriander; 1 teaspoon ground cummin; the seeds of six cardamoms; 1-inch stick of turmeric; $\frac{1}{2}$-inch stick of ginger; flesh of one coconut; 3 or 4 coriander leaves (optional); 1 teaspoon asafoetida (hing), 1-inch cinnamon; 1 tablespoon butter or cooking fat; 1 dessert-spoon cooking oil.

Halve, then soak, the aubergenes with the potatoes and carrots, in cold water. Mash the turmeric and ginger; break up the cinnamon finely and mix into a paste with coriander, cardamoms, cummin, garlic and chillis. Slice two onions finely in a tablespoon of butter or cooking fat and fry the spices in it. Scrape the flesh of the coconut, and add. If you can't get a coconut, use $\frac{1}{2}$ lb desiccated coconut.

Pour the cooking oil into a deep pan, heat and toss in the asafoetida; then add the mixed spices, coconut and coriander leaves. Add half a pint of water and bring to the boil. Now put in aubergenes, carrots, potatoes, tomato, beans (or peas), and two onions, halved. Bring to the boil once more, close with a well fitting lid and simmer till carrots and beans are soft. Most of the liquid should evaporate leaving a thick rich gravy. Eat with plain rice and pickle. Enough for four.

## How To Cook Rice

Rice to accompany curry should be dry and puffy, each grain separate from the others. Those who don't know how, produce a noxious, glutinous mess; yet boiled rice is one of the easiest dishes to make.

Fill a nine-inch saucepan with water about an inch from the rim. Take two tea cups of rice, rinse well and drain, then sprinkle into the water. Bring the water to the boil, then simmer and stir with a wooden spoon. In about twenty minutes the rice should be cooked through.

To ensure that it is cooked but not overdone, take out a grain or two and pinch between finger and thumb. If soft but firm, it is ready to be eaten. If the centres are hard, cook for a minute or two.

Now lift the pan into the sink and allow *cold* water to pour in *gently*, otherwise the rice will rise and spill into the sink. When about half the boiling water has been displaced by cold, pour into a colander, allow the water to run away, and shake gently. Empty into a warm dish and riffle gently with a fork. Allow the dish to stand either on the top of a hot oven, or inside a warm oven with the door ajar. It should be ready for serving in ten minutes.

### Vegetable Pilau (or Pilaf)

One breakfast cup long rice (Patna, Kashmir or Burma); 4-6 bay leaves; 4 medium size carrots; 2 large onions, finely sliced; 1 cup cauliflower heads; ¾ cup shelled peas; 5 tablespoons seedless raisins or sultanas; ¾ cup mixed peanuts, almonds, pine kernels, pistachios (or any other nuts); 2 tablespoons butter or cooking fat.

Wash rice and soak for an hour. Put 4 breakfast cups of water into a thick saucepan, add peas, carrots peeled and sliced, and cauliflower heads, cover and boil till tender but not soft; then strain off the liquid and keep for stock.

Heat half the fat and fry half the onions, finely sliced, and the nuts, till golden brown; then remove the pan.

Heat the remainder of the fat, put in the partly cooked vegetables, mix well but do not break them, and simmer for a minute or two. Remove from the heat.

Now put the drained rice into a pan with the hot fat, add the raisins, simmer and stir for two or three minutes, pour in the stock, and add bay leaves and salt, to taste. Bring to the boil, then turn down the heat, put on a close fitting lid and simmer till the rice is soft and the stock absorbed.

Mix rice and cooked vegetables together, empty into a serving dish and garnish with onions fried crisply, cashews and almonds and a sprig or two of parsley.

Any vegetables in season may be used, and if you eat meat, half a pound of chopped meat or chicken may be added. Pilaus are popular not only in India but in Egypt, Turkey, the Levant, Turkestan, Siberia and throughout the East.

### Panch Phoran (or Phora)

Curries need not be pungent but they should be tasty; and the spices need not be ground or roasted, but used in their natural state.

Great favourites are *panch phoras* (*panch* means five, and it is from this that the word punch is derived, because originally it consisted of five ingredients: brandy, gin, rum, tea and whisky).

The most popular *panch phoras* consist of equal quantities of mustard seed, aniseed, cummin, cassia leaves, and red chillis; and cummin seed, fenugreek, aniseed, mustard seed, and black cummin.

All you have to do is to add a teaspoon of *panch phora* to an onion finely sliced and fry this in fat or oil till the onions are golden brown, then add to a stew or pie; or you can add it without frying. A couple to whom I gave some *panch phora* now refuse to eat rabbit pie without it!

### Hulva or Hulwa

India, Turkey, and the East are noted for a sweet called *hulva* or *hulwa* which is made with a variety of ingredients. The simplest *hulva* is:

*Soojee Hulva*

*Soojee* is the Indian name for semolina, which as children we dislike so much perhaps because we've never been given it this way.

Two oz semolina; 2 oz butter; 2 oz Barbadoes (or Demerara) sugar; 1 oz blanched almonds; 1 oz sultanas; one teaspoon, ground cinnamon; the seeds of 12 cardamoms; one pint of water.

Add the sugar to the water, bring it to the boil, simmer for a minute, and pour into a jug.

Melt the butter in a 7-inch pan, add semolina and cook and stir till the semolina turns golden brown.

*Very slowly* add the syrup to the hot semolina, otherwise it will splutter and may burn you. Cook, mixing all the while, till the water is absorbed and the semolina swells. Add the sultanas, almonds, cardamom seeds and cinnamon as soon as the syrup has been poured in. The moment the mixture starts to stick, pour the contents of the pan into a flat dish and pat down level. May be eaten either warm or cold, with or without cream, though tastier when warm. Can be kept in the fridge and warmed as needed. Enough for four. Takes about half an hour to make, though it is best to have the almonds, cardamoms and sultanas ready before you start. Also made with carrots, marrow and other fruits and vegetables.

*Windsor Castle Carrot Pudding*

Gabriel Tschumi, Chef to the households of Queen Victoria and Queen Mary, says in his book *Royal Chef* that this was a favourite with the staff at Windsor Castle. We tried it and were pleasantly surprised to find how excellent it is, and unlike most steamed puddings, which are stodgy. It makes an appetising sweet on a cold winter's day. Five oz grated carrot; 5 oz self-raising wholemeal flour; $\frac{1}{4}$ oz vegetable fat; 2 oz currants; 3 oz Barbadoes sugar; 2 oz chopped raisins; $\frac{3}{4}$ cup chopped orange peel; $\frac{1}{4}$ teaspoon grated nutmeg; $\frac{3}{4}$ cup chopped orange peel; 1 egg; a little milk; $\frac{1}{2}$ teaspoon salt (optional).

Mix the dry ingredients in a bowl, then add the beaten egg and milk. Put into a greased pudding basin, cover with a cloth and steam for two hours and a quarter. Serve with custard made with milk and eggs or with a custard sauce.

### Vegetable Loaf

Two cups carrots; 2 cups left-over potatoes; 1 cup wholemeal breadcrumbs; 2 cups milk or vegetable stock; 3 tablespoons 100 per cent wholemeal flour; $\frac{1}{2}$ teaspoon black pepper; 1 cup cooked string beans; 1 large onion, finely chopped; 6 cloves garlic, chopped; 5 tablespoons butter or cooking fat; 2 eggs, slightly beaten; 1 cup grated cheese; 2 teaspoons *panch phora*; $\frac{1}{2}$ teaspoon salt (optional).

Melt fat in a large pan, add flour and onions, milk and seasoning, cook till thick and fold in the cheese. Remove from the heat and add eggs, well mixed.

Arrange beans, potatoes and carrots in alternate layers in a greased baking dish. Pour the cheese-and-onion sauce over them, top with breadcrumbs previously buttered and bake in a moderate oven for 30 minutes. Enough for six. Meat left over from the Sunday joint may be chopped small and added to the vegetables.

### Stuffed Aubergenes

Two aubergenes; $\frac{1}{4}$ teaspoon black pepper; $\frac{3}{4}$ cup wholemeal breadcrumbs; $\frac{1}{4}$ cup melted fat; 2 tablespoons chopped onion; 1 teaspoon lemon juice (or more); 1 cup chopped ham or nutmeat; $\frac{1}{2}$ cup vegetable or meat stock; 2 teaspoons *panch phora* (optional); $\frac{1}{2}$ teaspoon salt (optional).

Cut the tops off the aubergenes. Remove the pulp, leaving only a thin shell. Mash the pulp and mix with all the ingredients. Put the mixture into the empty shells, add the top pieces and bake in a moderate oven for 45 minutes. Enough for two.

## Potatoes Again

One never tires of potatoes. Big floury potatoes baked in their jackets and eaten with garlic, butter and a sprinkle of pepper freshly milled, make a satisfying meal. So do parsnips baked in their jackets, and baked beets taste much better than boiled. The baking of foods retains natural flavours.

## Aloo Dam (pronounced Ah-loo Daam)

This is a tasty Indian savoury made from *aloo* (potato) cooked slowly over a light heat (*dam*).

One lb new potatoes, large or small; ½ teaspoon *garam massala* (hot spices); ½ teaspoon ground turmeric; ½ teaspoon ground coriander; ¼ teaspoon red pepper; ¼ teaspoon black pepper; 3 cassia leaves; 2 oz yogurt; 4 oz butter or other fat; a pinch of aniseed; ½ teaspoon ground cummin; a pinch of dried ginger; salt to taste (optional).

Put the coriander, turmeric, pepper and ginger into a bowl and mix into a paste with a little water.

Scrub the potatoes and parboil them so that they are still firm. Mix the spice-paste with the yogurt and smear over the potatoes.

Melt the fat in a saucepan, add cassia leaves, aniseed, cummin and *garam massala*. Put in two or three tablespoons of water, mix; then drop the potatoes in and gently spoon the gravy over them. Simmer till the gravy is absorbed. This makes a supper snack for two.

## A Word About Salt

"On 6th September 1734," recorded the *Gentleman's Magazine*, "died in France the Sieur Michael Tourant, aged 98, of whom it is said that he never ate salt, and had none of the infirmities of old age."

Were there space I could write a chapter about the harm done by excessive salt—and one way and another, most people eat at least ½ oz of salt a day. Which is too much.